The Best of
British

THIS IS A PRION BOOK

First published in Great Britain in 2016 by Prion
An imprint of the Carlton Publishing Group
20 Mortimer Street
London W1T 3JW

A CIP catalogue for this book is available from the British Library.

ISBN 978-1-85375-959-8

Printed in Dubai

10 9 8 7 6 5 4 3 2 1

The Best of
British

Humorous and Inspirational Quotes
Celebrating What Makes Britain Great

PRION

Contents

Introduction	7
British... and Proud!	9
National Treasures	55
A Nice Cup of Tea	85
A United Kingdom	95
A Very British Sense of Humour	141

Introduction

Welcome to *The Best of British*, a collection of humorous quotations about Great Britain and what precisely makes it so great. It may be a tiny island, made up of four distinct nations (who often prefer to have nothing to do with each other!), but what the place lacks in size, it makes up for in style, wit and good old-fashioned eccentricity. Full of musings from famous Britons, as well declarations of affection from many of the world's greatest movers and shakers, *The Best of British* is exactly what it says on the tin.

Our sceptred isle has given the world so much, from roast beef sandwiches to the Beatles to the Internet – it really is the cat's pyjamas and the bee's knees.

So, without further much ado about nothing, let's pop the kettle on, make a brew, take a pew and keep calm and carry on…

British...
and Proud!

"However British you may be,
I am more British still."

Henry James

"British aren't really known for
their physical loveliness but firemen,
generally speaking, are gorgeous."

Emma Thompson

"'Do you mean to say that "so and so" was caught with a guardsman?'
'Yes, prime minister.'
'On a park bench?'
'Yes.'
'At 6 o'clock in the morning?'
'Yeah, that's right.'
'In this weather?'
'Yes, prime minster.'
'By God, man, it makes you proud to be British.'"

Winston Churchill

"There is nothing like staying at home for real comfort."

Jane Austen

"This is where I grew up. This is where I started life. This is my country and when I put on a Great Britain vest I'm proud. I'm very proud."

Mo Farah

"I do think Britain is a perfect size."

Bill Bryson

"I cannot lead you into battle.
I do not give you laws or administer
justice, but I can do something
else – I can give my heart and my
devotion to these old islands and
to all the peoples of our
brotherhood of nations."

Queen Elizabeth II

"To many, no doubt, he will
seem to be somewhat blatant and
bumptious, but we prefer to regard
him as being simply British."

Oscar Wilde

"We may be a small country,
but were a great one, too.
The country of Shakespeare,
Churchill, the Beatles, Sean
Connery, Harry Potter. David
Beckham's right foot. David
Beckham's left foot, come to that."

Richard Curtis

"But it is my happiness to be half
Welsh, and that the better half."

Richard Cobden

"This is my country,
The land that begat me,
These windy spaces
Are surely my own.
And those who here toil
In the sweat of their faces
Are flesh of my flesh
And bone of my bone."

Sir Alexander Gray

"The world is a place on which
England is found."

G.K. Chesterton

"We shall defend our island,
whatever the cost may be, we shall
fight on the beaches, we shall
fight on the landing grounds,
we shall fight in the fields and in
the streets, we shall fight in the hills;
we shall never surrender."

Winston Churchill

"This royal throne of kings,
this sceptred isle,
This earth of majesty, this seat
of Mars,
This other Eden, demi-paradise,
This fortress built by Nature
for herself
Against infection and the
hand of war,
This happy breed of men,
this little world,
This precious stone set in the
silver sea."

William Shakespeare

"You think the Welsh are friendly,
but the Irish are fabulous."

Bonnie Tyler

"I'm very proud to be British.
I'm very conscious of carrying my
country with me wherever I go.
I feel I need to represent it well."

Julie Andrews

"I think most of the world would like to be Scottish. All the Americans who come here never look for English blood or Welsh, only for Scottish and Irish. It's understandable. The Scots effectively created the face of the modern world: the railways, the bridges, the tunnels."

Joanna Lumley

"Be blind. Be stupid. Be British. Be careful."

Virginia Graham

"Britain, Britain, Britain...
it's been called Heaven on Earth
and it's easy to see why. Ribena is
plentiful, shoes laces are available in
different lengths and there's a new
Fred Bassett cartoon in the *Daily
Mail* every day. But let's not forget
the people of Britain for it is they
what make it good and nice.
Yippety doo–dah!"

Little Britain

"What Britain needs is an iron lady."

Margaret Thatcher

"The sayings of the Briton resound
with the wisdom of the heart and
sage comprehension of life."

Nikolai Gogol

"The sound of modern Britain
is a complex harmony, not a
male voice choir."

David Cameron

"Other nations use 'force';
we Britons alone use 'might'."

Evelyn Waugh

"It's a good time to be British,
especially for an artist. I wouldn't
say I'm proud to be British, but for
the first time, I'm not ashamed to
be British. Britishness is looking out
of a bus window, seeing sexy,
stylish people laughing."

Tracy Emin

"Where is the coward that would not dare to fight for such a land as Scotland?"

Walter Scott

"They (the British) are like their own beer; froth on top, dregs at bottom, the middle excellent."

Voltaire

"Should the invader come to Britain, there will be no placid lying down of the people in submission before him, as we have seen, alas! in other countries. We will defend every village, every town, and every city. The vast mass of London itself, fought street by street, could easily devour an entire hostile army, and we would rather see London laid in ashes and ruins than that it should be tamely and abjectly enslaved."

Winston Churchill

"Amazing what the British do
with language; the nuances of
politeness. The world's great
diplomats, surely?"

Anne Rice

"For such a small country, Britain
packs in an amazing diversity
of landscapes: coastline, lakes,
mountains, rolling countryside,
villages and great cities."

Rory Bremner

"The British are special. The world knows it. In our innermost thoughts we know it. This is the greatest nation on earth."

Tony Blair

"I rode over the mountains to Huddersfield (Yorkshire). A wilder people I never saw in England. The men, women and children filled the streets and seemed just ready to devour us."

John Wesley

"Scotland is one of the most
hauntingly beautiful places in the
world, the history is fascinating, the
men are handsome and the whisky
is delicious. But don't eat
the macaroni pies."

J.K. Rowling

"Britain's most useful role
is somewhere between bee
and dinosaur."

Harold MacMillan

"Milton! thou shouldst be living at
this hour:
England hath need of thee:
she is a fen
Of stagnant waters:
altar, sword, and pen,
Fireside, the heroic wealth of hall
and bower,
Have forfeited their ancient
English dower
Of inward happiness.
We are selfish men;
Oh! raise us up, return to us again;
And give us manners, virtue,
freedom, power.

William Wordsworth

"Remember that you are an Englishman, and have consequently won first prize in the lottery of life."

Cecil Rhodes

"Be Britain still to Britain true,
Amang oursels united;
For never but by British hands,
Maun British wrangs be righted."

Robert Burns

"Modest about our national pride – and inordinately proud of our national modesty."

Ian Hislop

"We are a small country with a large sense of its own importance."

David Walliams

"Why, why, why was I born an Englishman! – my cursed, rotten-boned, pappy-hearted countrymen, why was I sent to them?"

D.H. Lawrence

"The English have an extraordinary ability for flying into a great calm."

Alexander Woollcott

"I can't bear Britain in decline.
I just can't."

Margaret Thatcher

"I don't want to be Prime Minister
of England, I want to be Prime
Minister of the whole of the
United Kingdom."

David Cameron

"I know I have but the body of a weak and feeble woman; but I have the heart of a king, and of a king of England, too."

Queen Elizabeth I

"Britain is a world by itself, and we will nothing pay for wearing our own noses."

William Shakespeare

"There are many things in life
more worthwhile than money.
One is to be brought up in this
our England which is still the envy
of less happy lands."

Lord Denning

"The birth-place of valour, the
country of worth;
Wherever I wander, wherever I rove,
The hills of the Highlands for
ever I love."

Robert Burns

"Fifty years on from now, Britain will still be the country of long shadows on cricket grounds, warm beer, invincible green suburbs, dog lovers and pools fillers and, as George Orwell said, 'Old maids bicycling to holy communion through the morning mist' and, if we get our way, Shakespeare will still be read even in school."

John Major

"England is the paradise of women, the purgatory of men, and the hell of horses."

John Florio

"If the British Empire is fated to pass from life into history, we must hope it will not be by the slow process of dispersion and decay, but in some supreme exertion for freedom, for right and for truth."

Winston Churchill

"Britain is the only country in
the world where the food is more
dangerous than the sex."

Jackie Mason

"Correct English is the slang of
prigs who write history and essays.
And the strongest slang of all is the
slang of poets."

George Eliot

"Think of that, ye loyal Britons! We whalemen supply your kings and queens with coronation stuff!"

Herman Melville

"In the end it may well be that Britain will be honoured by historians more for the way she disposed of an empire than for the way in which she acquired it."

Lord Harlech

"We are the last people on earth, and the last to be free: our very remoteness in a land known only to rumour has protected us up till this day. Today the furthest bounds of Britain lie open – and everything unknown is given an inflated worth. But now there is no people beyond us, nothing but tides and rocks and, more deadly than these, the Romans."

Tacitus

"We do not regard the English as foreigners. We look on them only as rather mad Norwegians."

Halvard Lange

"Perdomita Britannia et statim omissa."
(Britain was conquered and immediately lost.)

Tacitus

"When people say England, they sometimes mean Great Britain, sometimes the United Kingdom, sometimes the British Isles – but never England."

George Mikes

"If there is a single trait in our character that has historically set us apart from other nations, it is our determination to limit the authority of those who rule over us."

Billy Bragg

"We have our own dream and our own task. We are with Europe, but not of it. We are linked but not combined."

Winston Churchill

"We might be a small country but we're a great one and the quirky list of British loves tells you something about our character."

William Hill

"The kingdom was formed to stand forth alone, and be distinguished from other nations."

John Butley

"The English are not very spiritual people, so they invented cricket to give them some idea of eternity."

George Bernard Shaw

"I would say to the House as
I said to those who have joined this
government: I have nothing to offer
but blood, toil, tears, and sweat…
You ask, what is our aim? I can
answer in one word: victory. Victory
at all costs − victory in spite of all
terror − victory, however long and
hard the road may be, for without
victory there is no survival."

Winston Churchill

"Patriotism is not enough,
I must have no hatred or
bitterness to anyone."

Edith Cavell

"England will still be England, an
everlasting animal, stretching into
the future and the past, and, like all
living things, having the power to
change out of all recognition and
yet remain the same."

George Orwell

"Europe is not to be saved by any single man. England has saved herself by her exertions, and will, as I trust, save Europe by her example."

William Pitt the Younger

"We had to do what we had to do – Britain is great again."

Margaret Thatcher

"The scum of the earth... but what
fine soldiers we have made them."

Duke of Wellington, on British soldiers

"The English certainly and
fiercely pride themselves in never
praising themselves."

Wyndham Lewis

"Hating Britain is a fundamental
part of being British."

Ben Mitchell

"The maxim of the British people
is business as usual."

Winston Churchill

"As a nation, the people of this
lovely island called Britain are
at the point where even one
honest politician could give us
a collective and conceptual
nervous breakdown."

Steve Merrick

"It was one of those perfect English
autumnal days which occur more
frequently in memory than in life."

P.D. James

"I have an image of what a British gentleman looks like, and that image finds real expression in Prince Charles. He is beyond fashion – he is an archetype of style."

Donatella Versace

"I like the fact that I have good old–fashioned British teeth with a big gap."

Georgia Jagger

"You can't generalise about an entire country, but I like the energy of British men."

Taylor Swift

"I love British cursing – the cadence of it, the joy in the sound of the words, and the vulgarity of it."

Christopher Moore

"To live in Wales is to be conscious
At dusk of the spilled blood
That went into the making of
the wild sky,
Dyeing the immaculate rivers
In all their courses."

R.S. Thomas

"The Welsh are not like any other
people in Britain, and they know
how separate they are. They are the
Celts, the tough little wine-dark race
who were the original possessors of
the island, who never mixed with
the invaders coming later from the
east, but were slowly driven into the
western mountains."
Laurie Lee

National
Treasures

"If you lead a country like Britain,
a strong country, a country which
has taken a lead in world affairs in
good times and in bad, a country
that is always reliable, then you have
to have a touch of iron about you."

Margaret Thatcher

"I just wish the world was twice as
big and half of it was
still unexplored."

David Attenborough

"I'm not claiming divinity.
I've never claimed purity of soul.
I've never claimed to have the
answers to life. I only put out songs
and answer questions as honestly as
I can… But I still believe in peace,
love and understanding."

John Lennon

"With every door that closes a
new one opens."

Alexander Graham Bell

"The best time to plan a book is
while you're doing the dishes."

Agatha Christie

"Britain's got talent, enormous
talent; that's very obvious."

Simon Cowell

"England expects that every
man will do his duty."

Horatio Nelson

"Ambition leads me not only farther
than any other man has been before
me, but as far as I think it possible
for man to go."

James Cook

"The important thing is not
what they think of me, but what
I think of them."

Queen Victoria

"A little nonsense now and then,
is cherished by the wisest men."

Roald Dahl

"I think Britishness has died off
in my lifetime and nothing has
replaced it. When I as a child, it was
Winston Churchill, beefeaters and
lots of pink on the globe. Now it's
an irrelevant concept. Personally,
I'm a Londoner living in Europe."

Jon Snow

"When one burns one's bridges,
what a very nice fire it makes."

Dylan Thomas

"All men are cremated equal."

Spike Milligan

"Britain's an island; its always
had a constant ebb and flow
of immigration – it makes it
a better place."

John Lydon

"Be like a duck. Calm on the surface, but always paddling like the dickens underneath."

Michael Caine

"It is not easy to walk alone in the country without musing upon something."

Charles Dickens

"The world is divided into two sorts
of people: those who divide the
world into two sorts of people and
those who do not. I fall resolutely
into the latter category."

Stephen Fry

"I am British. I love Britain for all
its faults and all its virtues."

Helen Mirren

"We are showing that Englishmen can still die with a bold spirit, fighting it out to the end."

Robert Falcon Scott

"The moment you doubt whether you can fly, you cease for ever to be able to do it."

J.M. Barrie

"If not actually disgruntled, he was far from being gruntled."

P.G. Wodehouse

"The only possible way there'd be an uprising in this country would be if they banned car boot sales and caravanning."

Victoria Wood

"How is the Empire?"

King George V, on his death bed

"It is a far, far better thing that
I do, than I have ever done; it is a
far, far better rest that I go to than
I have ever known."

Charles Dickens

"'Twas brillig, and the slithy toves
did gyre and gimble in the wabe."

Lewis Carroll

"I will not cease from mental fight,
Nor shall my sword sleep in my hand
Till we have built Jerusalem
In England's green and
pleasant land."

William Blake

"When I go out into the countryside
and see the sun and the green
and everything flowering,
I say to myself, 'Yes indeed,
all that belongs to me!'"

Henri Rousseau

"Courage is found in
unlikely places."

J.R.R. Tolkien

"If I should die, think only
this of me:
That there's some corner of
a foreign field
That is forever England."

Rupert Brooke

"Call me Diana,
not Princess Diana."

Diana

"You're just in time for a little
smackerel of something."

A.A. Milne

"Heaven take thy soul, and England
keep my bones!"

William Shakespeare

"The lowest and vilest alleys of
London do not present a more
dreadful record of sin than does the
smiling and beautiful countryside."

Sir Arthur Conan Doyle

"Britain: the land of embarrassment
and breakfast."

Julian Barnes

"Let us therefore brace ourselves
to our duties, and so bear ourselves
that if the British Empire and its
Commonwealth last for a thousand
years, men will still say, this
was their finest hour."

Winston Churchill

"I care for myself. The more
solitary, the more friendless, the
more unsustained I am, the more
I will respect myself."

Charlotte Brontë

"My proudest achievement has been
the success of the shows and artists
I have been involved with, because
they were made in Britain."

Simon Cowell

"What is our task? To make Britain
a fit country for heroes to live in."

David Lloyd George

"The whole strength of England lies in the fact that the enormous majority of the English people are snobs."

George Bernard Shaw

"What a pity it is that we have no amusements in England but vice and religion!"

Sydney Smith

"Say, Britain, could you ever boast,
Three poets in an age at most?
Our chilling climate hardly bears
A sprig of bays in fifty years."

Jonathan Swift

"To be or not to be:
that is the question."

William Shakespeare

"You never find an Englishman among the under-dogs – except in England, of course."

Evelyn Waugh

"I travelled among unknown men,
In lands beyond the sea:
Nor England! Did I know till then
What love I bore to thee."

William Wordsworth

"The English language is like London: proudly barbaric yet deeply civilised, too, common yet royal, vulgar yet processional, sacred yet profane."

Stephen Fry

"When I appear in public people expect me to neigh, grind my teeth, paw the ground and swish my tail – none of which is easy."

Princess Anne

"The British nation is unique.
They are the only people who like
to be told how bad things are, who
like to be told the worst."

Winston Churchill

"There are three kinds of lies: lies,
damned lies, and statistics."

Benjamin Disraeli

"Warriors! and where are
warriors found,
If not on martial Britain's ground?
And who, when waked with
note of fire,
Love more than they the
British lyre?"

Walter Scott

"Most of our people have never
had it so good."

Harold MacMillan

"I have to be seen to be believed."

Queen Elizabeth II

"I have brought you to the ring,
now dance if you can."

William Wallace

"Let valour end my life!"

Walter Raleigh

"One if by land, two if by sea."
Henry Wadsworth Longfellow

"It's celebrated in British culture
to be eccentric."
Paloma Faith

"Just give me Britain, so that I may
paint it with your colours, but with
my own brush."
Cicero

"I am happy now that Charles
calls on my bedchamber less
frequently than of old. As it is,
I now endure but two calls a week
and when I hear his steps outside
my door I lie down on my bed,
close my eyes, open my legs and
think of England."

Lady Alice Hillingdon

"All gardening is
landscape painting."

William Kent

"Britain is characterized not just
by its independence but, above all,
by its openness."

David Cameron

A Nice Cup of Tea

"The British have an umbilical cord which has never been cut and through which tea flows constantly. It is curious to watch them in times of sudden horror, tragedy or disaster. The pulse stops apparently, and nothing can be done, and no move made, until a nice cup of tea is quickly made. There is no question that it brings solace and does steady the mind. What a pity all countries are not so tea-conscious. World peace conferences would run more smoothly if a nice cup of tea or, indeed, a samovar were available at the proper time."

Marlene Dietrich

"In Britain, a cup of tea is the
answer to every problem.
Fallen off your bicycle?
Nice cup of tea."

David Walliams

"One cannot trust people whose
cuisine is so bad."

Jacques Chirac

"You can never get a cup of tea
large enough or a book long
enough to suit me."

C.S. Lewis

"What two ideas are more inseparable
than beer and Britannia?"

Sydney Smith

"Being British is about singing karaoke in bars, eating Chinese noodles and Japanese sushi, drinking French wine, wearing Prada and Nike, dancing to Italian house music, listening to Cher, using an Apple Mac, holidaying in Florida and Ibiza, and buying a house in Spain. Shepherds pie and going on holiday to Hastings went out about 50 years ago and the only people you'll see wearing a Union Jack are French movie stars or Kate Moss."

Malcolm McLaren

"Suddenly, in the space of a moment,
I realized what it was that I loved
about Britain – which is to say, all
of it. Every last bit of it, good and
bad – Marmite, village fetes, country
lanes, people saying 'mustn't grumble'
and 'I'm terribly sorry' but, people
apologizing to me when I conk
them with a nameless elbow, milk in
bottles, beans on toast, haymaking in
June, stinging nettles, seaside piers,
Ordnance Survey maps, crumpets,
hot-water bottles as a necessity, drizzly
Sundays – every bit of it."

Bill Bryson

"Roast beef, medium, is not only a food. It is a philosophy."

Edna Ferber

"When mighty Roast Beef was the Englishman's food,
It ennobled our brains and enriched our blood.
Our soldiers were brave and our courtiers were good
Oh! the Roast Beef of old England, And old English Roast Beef!"

Henry Fielding

"There are few hours in life more agreeable than the hour dedicated to the ceremony known as afternoon tea."

Henry James

"Tea! That's all I needed! Good cup of tea! Super-heated infusion of free-radicals and tannin, just the thing for healing the synapses."

Russell T. Davies

"When Britain first, at heavens
command,
Arose from out the azure main,
This was the charter of the land,
And guardian angels sung
this strain:
Rule, Britannia, rule the waves;
Britons never will be slaves."

James Thompson

A United
Kingdom

"There is not a single image of
Britishness. If Britishness is about
anything, it isn't about places
or people, its about institutions.
Britishness is parliamentary
democracy, rule of law, fairness and
decency. It is the institutions that
deliver this. It's not black, it's not
white, it's not the shires, it's
not London, it's not brassy and
it's not old-fashioned."

Michael Ignatieff

"Had we lived I should have had a tale to tell of the hardihood, endurance and courage of my companions which would have stirred the heart of every Englishman. These rough notes and our dead bodies must tell the tale."

Robert Falcon Scott

"We shall have to learn again to be one nation, or one day we shall be no nation."

Margaret Thatcher

"The English are not happy unless they are miserable, the Irish are not at peace unless they are at war, and the Scots are not at home unless they are abroad."

George Orwell

"Look at Scottish guys wearing kilts – you could look at them and laugh, but the way they carry themselves, how can you?"

André Benjamin

"If you are going through hell, keep going."

Winston Churchill

"Teaching the history of the British Empire links in with that of the world: for better and for worse, the Empire made us what we are, forming our national identity. A country that does not understand its own history is unlikely to respect that of others."

Antony Beevor

"Of all the small nations of this earth, perhaps only the ancient Greeks surpass the Scots in their contribution to mankind."

Winston Churchill

"Be England what she will, With all her faults she is my country still."

Charles Churchill

"England is a paradise for women and hell for horses; Italy is a paradise for horses, hell for women, as the proverb goes."

Robert Burton

"The British have always been madly overambitious, and from one angle it can seem like bravery, but from another it looks suspiciously like a lack of foresight."

Ben Aaronovitch

"We are a naturally pragmatic people. We know how to take the influence of the likes of Scott and Austen and turn them into new things. I am tired of the frontline of swinging Britain – it's false and artificial and has nothing to do with our inventive art, music and fashion. I don't think we care about cream teas and old maids on bikes, but we do love our landscape."

A.S. Byatt

"Britishness is a complicated and enormous thing – what different people see as meaning different things. It can mean one island, a group of islands off the coast of Europe, or it can mean the British Empire – at times it means all those things. Politicians, and the rest of us, define it in different ways at different times."

David Cannadine

"I think what is British about me
is my feelings and awareness of
others and their situations. English
people are always known to be well
mannered and cold, but we are not
cold – we don't interfere in your
situation. If we are heartbroken, we
don't scream in your face with tears
– we go home and cry on our own."

Michael Caine

"The British Isles are awash with the choice of beautiful historic churches, abbeys, and cathedrals where one king or another has tied the knot and bestowed a royal precedent."

Tina Brown

"I'm three quarters Scottish, but I sound English. I don't really see British as a race."

Joanna Lumley

"I feel more Irish than English.
I feel freer than British, more
visceral, with a love of language.
Shot through with fire in some
way. That's why I resist being
appropriated as the current
repository of Shakespeare on the
planet. That would mean I'm part
of the English cultural elite, and
I am utterly ill–fitted to be."

Kenneth Branagh

"The French and the British are such good enemies that they can't resist being friends."

Peter Ustinov

"Anything said in upper-crust British automatically sounds intelligent."

Nancy Kress

"God help England if she had no
Scots to think for her."

George Bernard Shaw

"Each section of the British Isles
has its own way of laughing, except
Wales, which doesn't."

Stephen Leacock

"Anyone that knows me knows what I'm about, and I'm very much a British actor."

Robert Carlyle

"British people have a strong sense of what is fair."

George Osborne

"I am very British. We don't like
to be pushed around."

Damon Hill

"There is a marvelous turn and
trick to British arrogance; its
apparent unconsciousness makes
it twice as effectual."

Catherine Drinker Bowen

"Britain is not a country that is easily rocked by revolution… in Britain our institutions evolve. We are a Fabian society writ large."

William Hamilton

"I like the English. They have the most rigid code of immorality in the world."

Malcolm Bradbury

"Dear Land of Hope,
thy hope is crowned.
God make thee mightier yet!
On Sov'ran brows,
beloved, renowned,
Once more thy crown is set.
Thine equal laws, by
Freedom gained,
Have ruled thee well and long;
By Freedom gained, by
Truth maintained,
Thine Empire shall be strong."

A.C. Benson

"You British plundered half the
world for your own profit.
Let's not pass it off as the Age
of Enlightenment."

Paddy Chayefsky

"When a man is tired of London,
he is tired of life; for there is in
London all that life can afford."

Samuel Johnson

"This England never did,
nor never shall,
Lie at the proud foot of
a conqueror,
But when it first did help to
wound itself.
Now these her princes are
come home again,
Come the three corners of the
world in arms,
And we shall shock them.
Nought shall make us rue,
If England to itself do rest
but true."

William Shakespeare

"Ireland is the home of men who are complete savages and lead a miserable existence because of the cold; and therefore, in my opinion, the northern limit of our inhabited world is to be placed there."

Strabo

"The English feel *schadenfreude* even about themselves."

Martin Amis

"You know what the Englishman's idea of compromise is? He says, 'Some people say there is a God. Some people say there is no God.' The truth probably lies somewhere between these two statements."

William Butler Yeats

"We have always found the Irish a bit odd. They refuse to be English."

Winston Churchill

"The debate about Britishness is promoted by the extent of our post-war decline. We are no longer kept together by the need to fight wars, we are no longer all Protestants and we do not have the self-interest of belonging to a massive global empire."

Linda Colley

"I'm leaving because the weather is too good. I hate London when it's not raining."

Groucho Marx

"America has no truer friend than Great Britain. Once again, we are joined together in a great cause – so honoured the British Prime Minister has crossed an ocean to show his unity of purpose with America. Thank you for coming, friend."

George W. Bush

"I don't want to be Caesar, stroll about among the Britons and endure the Scythian winters."

Lucius Annaeus Florus

"I think it has something to do with being British. We don't take ourselves as seriously as some other countries do. I think a lot of people take themselves far too seriously; I find that a very tedious attitude."

Joan Collins

"Banner of England,
not for a season,
O Banner of Britain, hast thou
Floated in conquering battle or
flapt to the battle-cry!
Never with mightier glory than
when we had rear'd thee on high
Flying at top of the roofs in the
ghastly siege of Lucknow –
Shot thro' the staff or the halyard,
but ever we raised thee anew,
And ever upon the topmost roof our
banner of England blew."

Alfred Tennyson

"When its three o'clock in New York, it's still 1938 in London."

Bette Midler

"Our tolerance is part of what makes Britain Britain. So conform to it, or don't come here."

Tony Blair

"Britishness is the countryside,
individual liberty, unbroken
tradition, and no revolutions.
It is a country of poetry."

Shirley Williams

"You have sat too long for any
good you have been doing. Depart,
I say; and let us have done with you.
In the name of God, go!"

Oliver Cromwell

"An Englishman is a person who does things because they have been done before. An American is a person who does things because they haven't been done before."

Mark Twain

"I was born a Scotsman and a bare one. Therefore I was born to fight my way in the world."

Walter Scott

"Throughout the whole of England the drinking of tea is general. You have it twice a day and though the expense is considerable, the humblest peasant has his tea, just like the rich man."

Francois de La Rochefoucauld

"London – a place you go to get bronchitis."

Fran Lebowitz

"Some talk of Alexander,
And some of Hercules.
Of Hector and Lysander,
And such great names as these.
But of all the world's great heroes,
There's none that can compare
With the tow-row-row-row-row-row
Of the British grenadiers!"

Traditional marching song

"I fall in love with Britain every day,
with bridges, buses, blue skies...
but it's a brutal world, man."

Pete Doherty

"It's not that the Irish are cynical. It's rather that they have a wonderful lack of respect for everything and everybody."

Brendan Behan

"The most stirring battle-poem in English is about a brigade of cavalry which charged in the wrong direction."

George Orwell

"What an idiotic Yorkshireman thinks is British is not what some cultured southerner thinks. There is no one type of Britishness."

Brian Sewell

"Chicken masala is now Britain's true national dish, not only because it is the most popular, but because it is a perfect illustration of the way Britain absorbs and adapts external influences."

Robin Cook

"Only in Britain could it be
thought a defect to be too clever
by half. The probability is that too
many people are too stupid
by three-quarters."

John Major

"Britannia needs no bulwarks
No towers along the steep;
Her march is oer the
mountain wave,
Her home is on the deep."

Thomas Campbell

"There is no other Parliament like the English. For the ordinary man, elected to any senate, from Persia to Peru, there may be a certain satisfaction in being elected... but the man who steps into the English Parliament takes his place in a pageant that has ever been filing by since the birth of English history... York or Lancaster, Protestant or Catholic, court or country, Roundhead or Cavalier, Whig or Tory, Liberal or Conservative, Labour or Unionist, they all fit into that long pageant that no other country in the world can show."

Josiah Wedgwood

"Oh, to be in England
Now that April's there,
And whoever wakes in England
Sees, some morning, unaware,
That the lowest boughs and
the brushwood sheaf
Round the elm-tree bole are
in tiny leaf,
While the chaffinch sings on
the orchard bough
In England – now!"

Robert Browning

"Let us therefore brace ourselves to our duties, and so bear ourselves that, if the British Empire and its Commonwealth last for a thousand years, men will still say, 'This was their finest hour.'"

Winston Churchill

"Hearts at peace, under an English heaven."

Rupert Brooke

"Many people die of thirst, but the Irish are born with one."

Spike Milligan

"People define themselves as coming from Yorkshire or Lancaster, or as being cockney, like I am, rather than coming from Britain as a whole. There's a certain snottiness in trying to define Britishness. If anybody asked, I would say I am a Londoner and a European."

Claire Rayner

"The Irish is one race of people for whom psychoanalysis is of no use whatsoever."

Sigmund Freud

"An Englishman never enjoys himself, except for a noble purpose."

Alan Patrick Herbert

"I suppose an essential aspect of being British is not liking others very much. We are set apart by our lack of French-ness, German-ness or Italian-ness. Still, Britain is one of the few places left in the world which still has real beer."

Terry Jones

"Mad dogs and Englishmen go out in the midday sun."

Noel Coward

"We should abandon the idea of Britishness and acknowledge that we're really talking about what it means to be English. Scotland has its own identity."

Derek Draper

"We look to Scotland for all our ideas of civilization."

Voltaire

"An Englishman thinks seated; a
Frenchman, standing; an American,
pacing; an Irishman, afterward."

Austin O'Malley

"This country is epitomized by
surprise – nothing is as you expect it
to be. Unlike a police state, there is
a tradition of allowing eccentricity
and variety in Britain."

U.A. Fanthorpe

"An Englishman is a man who
lives on an island in the North Sea
governed by Scotsmen."

Philip Guedalla

"The stately homes of England!
How beautiful they stand,
Amidst their tall ancestral trees,
O'er all the pleasant land!"

Felicia Dorothea Hemans

"Where Napoleon failed,
I shall succeed, I shall land on
the shores of Britain."

Adolf Hitler

"I am Scottish. I am also British."

Andy Murray

"England is a nation
of shopkeepers."

Napoleon Bonaparte

A Very
British Sense
of Humour

"I used to go missing a lot...
Miss Canada, Miss United
Kingdom, Miss World."

George Best

"The British are the only people in
history crass enough to have made
revolutionaries out of Americans."

Shashi Tharoor

"An Englishman, even if he is alone,
forms an orderly queue of one."

George Mikes

"My folks were English...
we were too poor to be British."

Bob Hope

"I don't know what London's
coming to – the higher the buildings
the lower the morals."

Noël Coward

"It sometimes occurs to me that the British have more heritage than is good for them."

Bill Bryson

"Americans assume all British people have at least one servant."

Martin Freeman

"The British do not expect
happiness. I had the impression,
all the time that I lived there, that
they do not want to be happy;
they want to be right."

Quentin Crisp

"The feeling of friendship is like
that of being comfortably filled
with roast beef; love, like being
enlivened with champagne."

Samuel Johnson

"The way to endure summer in England is to have it framed and glazed in a comfortable room."

Horace Walpole

"Something is happening to Britain and the British. Or has happened. We are said to be passing through a transition, or a turning point, or a transformation; nobody is quite sure which."

Ferdinand Mount

"Nearly every woman in England
is competent to write an
authoritative article on how
not to cook cabbage."

Vyvyan Holland

"There'll always be an England...
even if it's in Hollywood."

Bob Hope

"The reason why Englishmen are the best husbands in the world is because they want to be faithful. A Frenchman or an Italian will wake up in the morning and wonder what girl he will meet. An Englishman wakes up and wonders what the cricket score is."

Barbara Cartland

"The English never smash in a face. They merely refrain from asking it to dinner."

Margaret Halsey

"If England treats her criminals the way she has treated me, she doesn't deserve to have any."

Oscar Wilde

"Ireland sober is Ireland stiff."

James Joyce

"Give me Scotland or I die!"

John Knox

"On the continent people have good food; in England people have good table manners."

George Mikes

"If the French were really intelligent, they'd speak English."

Wilfred Sheed

"The Englishman has all the qualities of a poker except its occasional warmth."

Daniel O'Connell

"In England there are sixty different religions, and only one sauce."

Francesco Caracciolo

"Continental people have sex lives; the English have hot-water bottles."

George Mikes

"No one can be as calculatedly rude as the British, which amazes Americans, who do not understand studied insult and can only offer abuse as a substitute."

Paul Gallico

"This Englishwoman is so refined,
She has no bosom and no behind."

Stevie Smith

"Those comfortably padded
lunatic asylums which are known,
euphemistically, as the stately
homes of England."

Virginia Woolf

"England has already lost the war. It is only a matter of having the intelligence to admit it."

Adolf Hitler

"Britishness… is also drunken yobs following a football team. It's patriotism which verges upon nationalism if encouraged."

Julian Critchley

"The English country gentleman galloping after a fox – the unspeakable in full pursuit of the uneatable."

Oscar Wilde

"There's only two things I hate in this world. People who are intolerant of other people's cultures and the Dutch."

Michael Caine

"There are only three things against living in Britain: the place, the climate and the people."

Jimmy Edwards

"The ability for us to laugh at ourselves is Britain's saving grace."

Martin Parr

"All British castles and old country homes are supposed to be haunted. It's in the lease."

Bob Hope

"There are two seasons in Scotland. June and winter."

Billy Connolly

"Heaven is where the police are British, the lovers French, the mechanics German, the chefs Italian, and it is all organized by the Swiss."

Famous proverb

"I've always felt more British than Irish. Maybe it was the way I was brought up, but I have always felt more of a connection with the UK than with Ireland."

Rory McIlroy

"I am Irish by race, but the English have condemned me to talk the language of Shakespeare."

Oscar Wilde

"Oats. A grain, which in England is generally given to horses, but in Scotland supports the people."

Samuel Johnson

"British women can't cook."

Prince Philip

"It is never difficult to distinguish between a Scotsman with a grievance and a ray of sunshine."

P.G. Wodehouse